SKILL BUILDER
SCIENCE

LEVEL
4

PUFFIN BOOKS

An imprint of Penguin Random House

PUFFIN BOOKS

USA | Canada | UK | Ireland | Australia
New Zealand | India | South Africa | China | Singapore

Puffin Books is part of the Penguin Random House group of companies
whose addresses can be found at global.penguinrandomhouse.com

Published by Penguin Random House India Pvt. Ltd
4th Floor, Capital Tower 1, MG Road,
Gurugram 122 002, Haryana, India

First published in Puffin Books by Penguin Random House India 2019

Text, design and illustrations copyright © Quadrum Solutions Pvt. Ltd 2019
Series copyright © Penguin Random House India 2019

ISBN 9780143445142

Design and layout by Quadrum Solutions Pvt. Ltd
Printed at Repro India Limited

www.penguin.co.in

Dear Moms and Dads,

There's no better way to prepare your children for their future than to equip them with all the skills they need to grow into confident adults. The Skill Builder series has been created to hone subject skills as well as twenty-first century skills so that children develop not just academic skills but also life skills.

The books in the Skill Builder series focus on numerical, science and English language skills. Recognizing that children learn best while having fun, the books in this series have been created with a high 'fun' quotient. Each subject is dealt with across four levels, so you can choose the level that best suits your child's learning stage.

The Skill Builder: Science books have been created by academic experts who have devised a special chart to help you track the skills your child needs to master in order to understand and apply science concepts.

It has been great creating this series with my highly charged Quadrum team—our academic experts, Noella Nazareth and Naimisha Sanghavi, who spent hours crafting each page; Himani, who designed every page to be a visual treat; Gopi, who painstakingly laid out every word; Bishnupriya and Ruby, who read and re-read every word; and Kunjli, who was the conscience of the entire series. And of course, the Puffin team—Sohini and Ashwitha—who added value at every step. When you have a great team, you're bound to have a great book.

I do hope you and your child enjoy the series as much as we have enjoyed creating it.

Sonia Mehta
PS: We'd love your feedback, so do write in to us at
funlearningbooks@quadrumltd.com

THE SKILL CHART

Here is a snapshot of the skills your child will acquire as they complete the activities.

- **Investigative or enquiry skills:** The ability to find information by looking for it in the right places.
- **Research skills:** The ability to examine and evaluate the usefulness of existing information with a specific objective or question in mind.
- **Observation skills:** The ability to carefully observe something and take note of important details or changes.
- **Communication skills:** The ability to structure and present thoughts and observations in a clear and precise manner.
- **Experimentation skills:** The ability to perform a procedure according to a set of instructions or parameters.
- **Inference or conclusion skills:** The ability to analyse the evidence and arrive at a rational conclusion.
- **Creative thinking skills:** The ability to view a problem creatively from different angles.
- **Critical thinking/problem solving skills:** Rationalizing, analysing, evaluating and interpreting information to make informed judgments.

Page no		Investigating/ Enquiry	Research	Observation	Explanation/ Communication	Experimentation	Inference/ conclusion	Creative thinking	Critical thinking
4	WHAT'S EDIBLE?	☺		☺					☺
5	MATCH ME!	☺							☺
6	SENSATIONAL SENSES	☺	☺	☺				☺	☺
7	RAINBOW FOODS	☺	☺	☺			☺	☺	☺
8	WATCH THEM GROW!	☺	☺	☺				☺	
10	INSECT WATCH	☺	☺	☺	☺				☺
11	SAFETY FIRST			☺	☺				
12	DIFFERENT COVERS	☺		☺			☺		☺
13	MATERIAL MAGIC	☺	☺				☺		☺
14	TASTING TIME	☺	☺			☺	☺	☺	
15	FRICTION!			☺			☺		☺
16	WHAT YOU EAT	☺	☺	☺					
17	OUR COMPLEX BODY	☺	☺				☺		☺
18	KNOW YOUR PLANTS	☺	☺		☺		☺	☺	☺

#	Activity
19	AM I EATING HEALTHY?
20	HOUSE BUILDERS
22	POSTER TIME
23	NOT QUITE ALIVE
24	CANDLELIGHT
26	ARE WE ALIKE?
27	COLOURFUL CORAL
28	CLEVER CACTUS
29	KNOW YOUR WATER CYCLE
30	WHAT'S THE NAME?
31	LET'S EXPLORE
32	ROCKS AND MINERALS
34	NIGHT WATCHMAN
35	PHYSICAL OR CHEMICAL?
36	WHO AM I?
37	FUEL UP!
38	SEED TRAVELS
40	LET IT SNOW
41	WE CARE
42	WHERE'S YOUR BACKBONE?
43	PARTICLE MATTERS
44	TOOTH TRUTHS
46	BE NATURAL
47	HEALTHY METHODS
48	BREATHE IN
49	GASES GALORE
50	ENERGY FORMS
51	MATERIAL CHECK
52	BRILLIANT BUGS
53	NOT SO SIMPLE
54	CREATING CONSTELLATIONS
56	ATTRACTION EXPLAINED
57	POWER SOURCE
58	WATER HOMES

The skills outlined in the above chart are the main skills children acquire as they do these activities. There are additional supplementary skills they will also learn that are not outlined here.

WHAT'S EDIBLE?

The fruits and vegetables we eat are all different parts of plants. Do you know which ones are roots and which ones are flowers, stems or leaves? Circle the odd one out in each category.

root	carrot	radish	potato	beet

stem	asparagus	beet	sugarcane	celery

leaf	lettuce	spinach	cabbage	cauliflower

flower	cauliflower	broccoli	artichoke	pear

seed	almond	pineapple	walnut	corn

fruit	banana	apple	pear	turnip

4

MATCH ME!

Where in the human body would you find the following?

alveoli •   •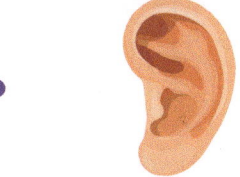

villi •   •

cerebrum •   •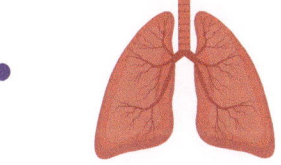

cornea •   •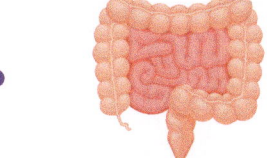

enamel •   •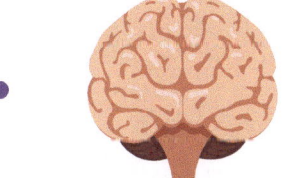

cochlea •   •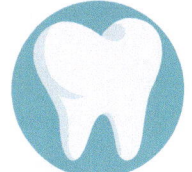

haemoglobin •   •

SENSATIONAL SENSES

Our sense organs help us experience the world around us through touch, taste, smell, hearing or sight. Can you match each word in the box to the correct sense?

salty	smooth	thunder	colour	bitter
music	beauty	whisper	rough	odour

Sight

Hearing

Taste

Touch

Smell

RAINBOW FOODS

Fruits and vegetables of different colours contain varied vitamins, nutrients and pigments that keep us healthy. Draw fruits and vegetables of different colours in the sections of the wheel below. One has been done for you.

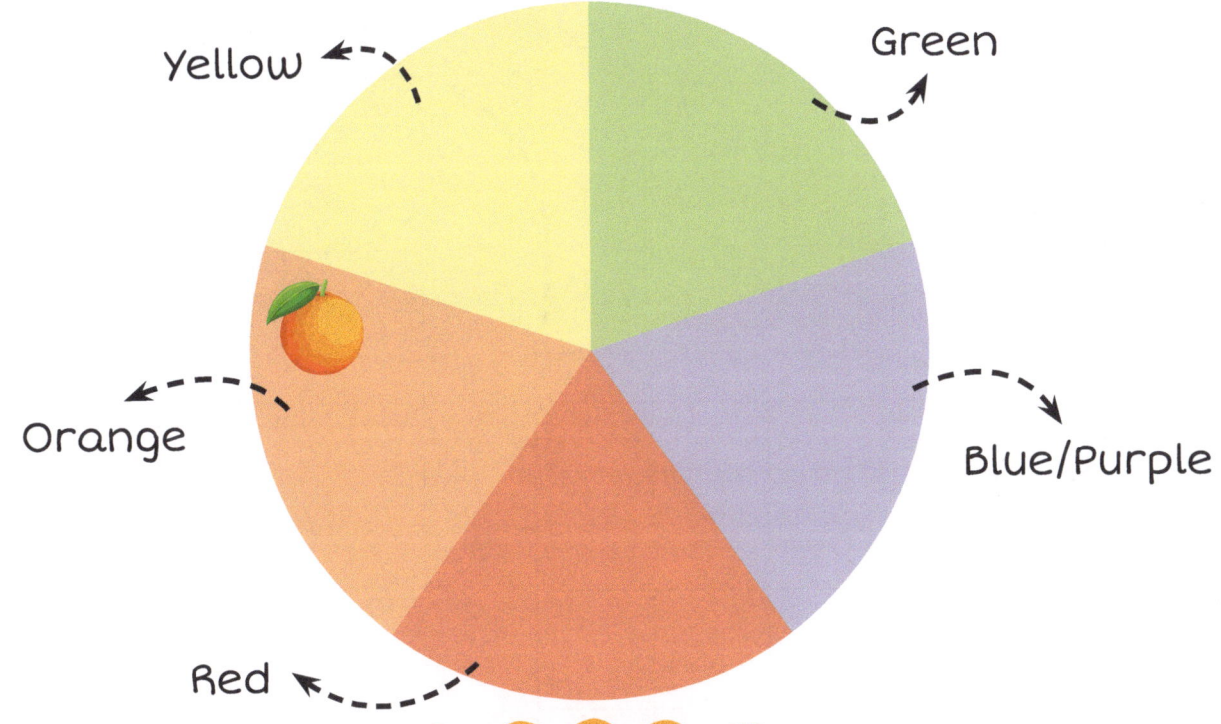

Look this up: Write down three reasons why one of the vegetables or fruits you drew is good for health.

_____

_____

_____

WATCH THEM GROW!

Growth is one of the characteristics of living things. Use the grids to help this flower grow in size.

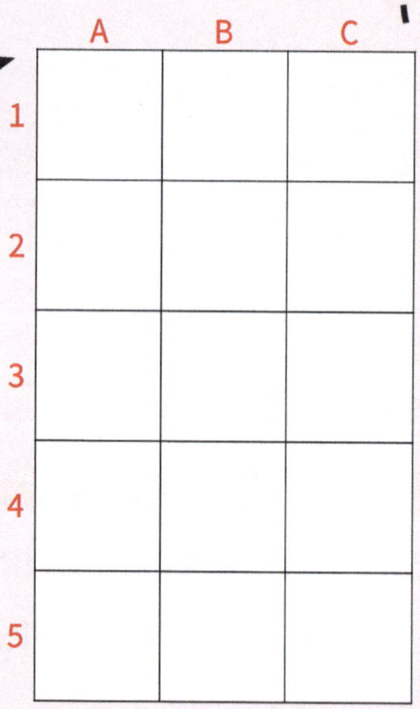

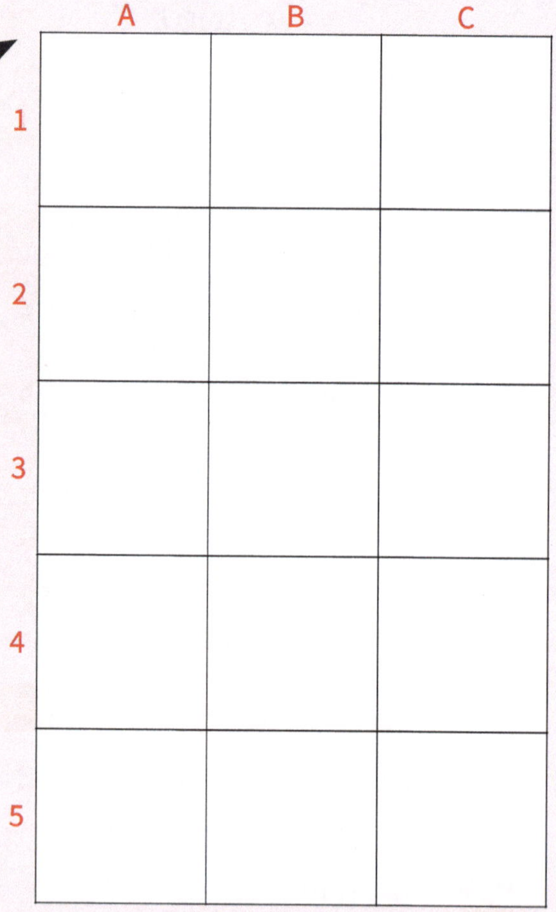

Have you ever seen a mason building a wall? He puts one brick on top of another and makes the wall increase in size!

Look this up: Is the wall a living thing? Why/Why not? _____
_____

Draw one living thing and one non-living thing in the spaces below. Show how each can grow.

Living thing

Non-living thing

INSECT WATCH

Identify four different insects that you have seen around the house or garden. Take pictures of them or draw them, find out an interesting fact about each and fill in the table below. Remember: Do not touch any insects with your bare hands.

Drawing	Name	Location (Where did you see it?)	Description (colour, size, shape, wings/ without wings)	Interesting facts about the insect
Insect 1				
Insect 2				
Insect 3				
Insect 4				

SAFETY FIRST

Here are some situations that could be dangerous. Describe what is happening in each one and explain why it might be dangerous.

Situation	Description	Why is it dangerous?

It is important to follow the rules to stay safe at all times!

DIFFERENT COVERS

Animals have lots of different types of skin coverings that help to keep them warm, cool or protected. What kind of skin coverings do these animals have?
Tick (✓) the right column.

	Fur	Feathers	Scales	Shell	Spines
emu					
tortoise					
tiger					
flamingo					
hedgehog					
fish					
snail					
cobra					
polar bear					
porcupine					

MATERIAL MAGIC

Materials have different properties. Depending on these properties, they have different uses. Find out more by filling in the blanks with words from the box.

> soft   tough   stiff   waterproof   flexible
> hardest   absorbs   brittle

1. Diamonds, the _____ substance on Earth, are used in cutting and drilling tools.

2. Bulletproof jackets are made from Kevlar because it is a _____ material.

3. Clay is _____, which allows you to mould it with your hands.

4. If your teacher drops a piece of chalk while writing on the board, it breaks because it is very _____.

5. Rubber is _____ and bends easily, wood is _____ and cannot bend.

6. Cotton is a good material to wear in summer as it _____ sweat.

7. Raincoats and rainwear are made from plastic because it is _____.

TASTING TIME

How do you know that something is very tasty? You taste it with the taste buds on your tongue.

Look this up: Butterflies have a unique way of tasting things. Find out how!

_____

Now draw a second butterfly in the empty grid and colour both.

FRICTION!

Friction is a force that operates between an object and the surface it is sliding over. This force slows down the movement of the object. Move a toy car on different surfaces. Measure the distance it travels before it stops. Then write down your observations in the chart below.

Surface	Distance travelled (measure using a tape measure or ruler)	More/Less Friction
smooth floor		
lawn		
pavement		
carpet		
glass table top		

Circle the correct answer.

1 The car travels faster on a smooth surface because there is **more/less** friction.

2 The car travels slower on a rough surface because there is **more/less** friction.

WHAT YOU EAT

Fruits and vegetables are packed with nutrients. If we don't include them in our daily diet, we could end up getting a disease caused by the deficiency of a vitamin or mineral (a deficiency is a lack or shortage of something). Match each nutrient to the disease its deficiency causes.

Vitamin A •   • scurvy

iodine •   • rickets

Vitamin B •   • anaemia

Vitamin D •   • beriberi

Vitamin C •   • night blindness

iron •   • goitre

OUR COMPLEX BODY

The human body is like a complex machine with different parts. The parts all work together to help the body function efficiently. Circle the odd one out in each group.

One has been done for you.

1. heart   (ears)   artery   vein

2. eyes   nose   liver   ear

3. skull   rib   femur   heart

4. toe   wrist   knee   ankle

5. mouth   stomach   kidney   intestine

6. nose   liver   lung   trachea

7. finger   arm   knee   shoulder

KNOW YOUR PLANTS

How well do you know your plants? Let's find out. Solve this crossword.

ACROSS

4 Part of the plant that contains the seed.
5 The name of the pigment that makes leaves green.
6 The kitchen of a plant.

DOWN

1 They anchor a plant in soil.
2 The tiny openings on leaves through which gases enter.
3 Insects help transfer this from one flower to the next.
4 The most colourful part of a plant.

AM I EATING HEALTHY?

Here are two pyramids. In Pyramid 1, write down the names of all foods that you eat rarely, sometimes and every day. In Pyramid 2, write down the names of foods that you should eat rarely, sometimes and every day in order to stay healthy!

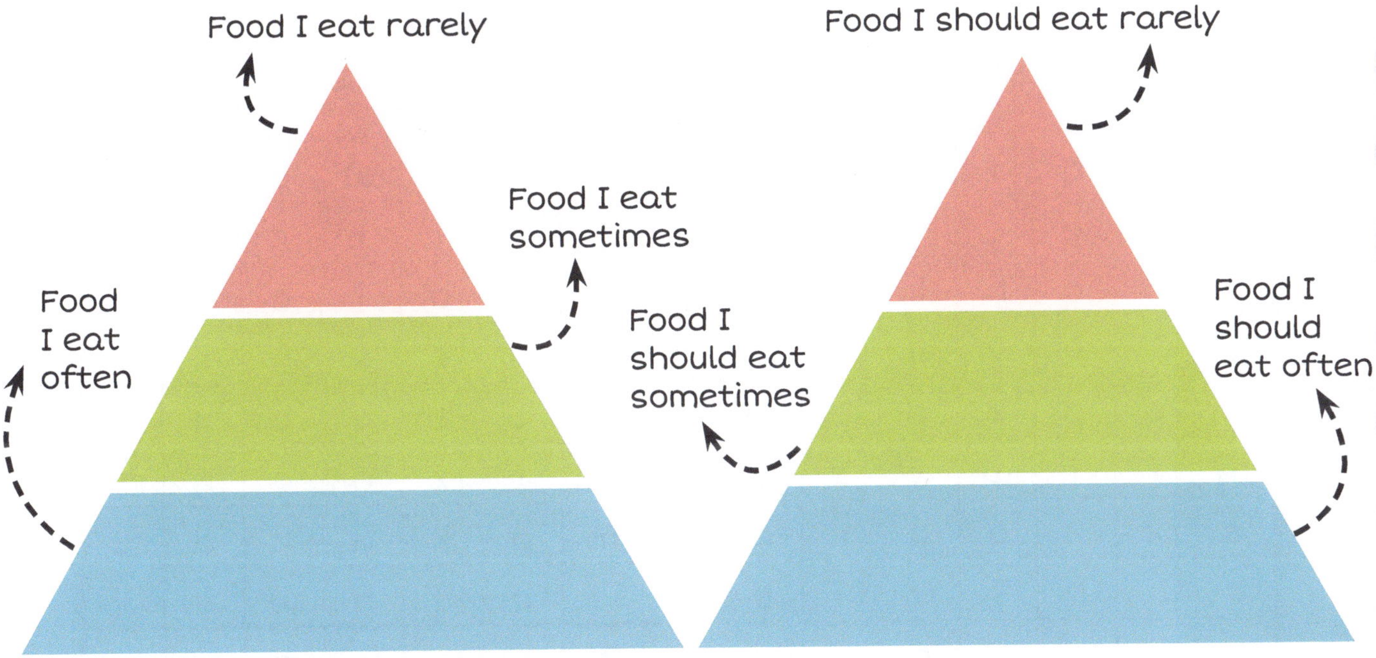

Food I eat rarely

Food I eat sometimes

Food I eat often

Pyramid 1

Food I should eat rarely

Food I should eat sometimes

Food I should eat often

Pyramid 2

Look this up: Is there a difference between the two pyramids? What is the difference?

_____

_____

HOUSE BUILDERS

Different materials are used not only to build houses but to furnish them as well. Furnishing a house includes adding light fixtures, bathroom fixtures, tiles, flooring, furniture, and so on. Find these building materials in the grid.

wood   concrete   steel   aluminium   glass
plastic   fabric   marble   bricks

c	a	q	i	m	b	r	i	c	k	s	w	o	o	d
h	i	c	c	t	j	g	k	y	k	i	x	r	v	x
s	o	q	h	k	o	g	p	u	g	p	i	c	m	p
z	i	v	y	u	f	p	g	l	a	s	s	h	z	l
w	p	p	x	r	a	m	n	f	l	l	q	b	n	a
m	f	i	w	l	b	j	a	r	j	x	o	o	h	s
a	x	k	o	p	r	g	z	m	p	k	n	r	a	t
r	a	n	j	m	i	b	h	l	c	c	p	w	l	i
b	s	c	o	n	c	r	e	t	e	r	l	n	u	c
l	f	y	x	i	p	v	g	t	t	s	n	j	m	o
e	h	x	m	w	o	a	c	z	q	u	b	c	i	x
j	r	u	y	q	j	h	y	w	w	h	h	u	n	u
t	e	z	p	q	d	u	h	t	y	j	m	y	i	d
o	s	t	e	e	l	w	f	q	x	u	s	h	u	x
i	c	e	k	l	a	u	n	q	z	i	r	p	m	d

20

Now write down where these building materials could be used in a house.

Material	Where it is used?
wood	
concrete	
steel	
aluminium	
bricks	
plastic	
fabric	
marble	
glass	

POSTER TIME

Reduce (cut down), reuse (find a new way to use it again) and recycle (make something new from something old) are three ways in which you could help to save our beautiful planet! Make your own poster on the three Rs.

Draw here.

NOT QUITE ALIVE

A bird is a living thing but the nest it lives in is a non-living thing. A bird's egg has some of the characteristics of a non-living thing, but under certain conditions, it will change into a living thing. The same is true of a seed. Fill in the table below based on what you know of eggs, seeds and the conditions under which they transform into living things.

	Non-living characteristics	Conditions required for transformation	Living characteristics after the change
Egg			
Seed			

CANDLELIGHT

What does the wick of a candle need in order to burn?
It needs a gas called oxygen that is present in the air.
Let's find out how necessary oxygen is for a candle to burn.

Adult supervision required

What you need

- a large glass jar
- two candles (one should be shorter than the glass jar)
- a matchbox
- a metal tray

Here's what you do

- Affix both candles onto the metal tray.

- Light both candles using matches.

- After a few moments, cover the second candle with the glass jar.

What happens to both candles?

_____

_____

_____

Draw your observations and write your inference in the space below:

Covered Candle

Observation:

Inference
Why did the candle continue to burn/ not burn?

Uncovered Candle

Observation:

Inference
Why did the candle continue to burn/ not burn?

ARE WE ALIKE?

Find two different types of plants, such as a tree and a shrub, or a tree and a herb. Find out what they are called. Examine them carefully and then write down five differences between them in the table below.

	Difference 1	Difference 2	Difference 3	Difference 4	Difference 5
Name of Tree					
Name of Plant					

COLOURFUL CORAL

The ocean is home to a variety of fish, marine plants, animals and colonies of tiny organisms called polyps. These colonies are colourful and beautiful and they are called coral. Many different types of corals make up a coral reef. Find ten differences between these two images.

Name two underwater organisms that you see in the picture.

_____   _____

The world's largest coral reef is the _____

_____ along the

coast of _____.

CLEVER CACTUS

Cacti can tolerate extreme heat and lack of water because they are adapted to survive in the desert. Unscramble the letters to learn how they adapt to a desert climate.

1. Cacti have thorns instead of _____ VLEASE to prevent loss of water from leaf surfaces.

2. Their stems are green and can carry out _____ TPHOSOHYNTSESI.

3. Their bodies are thick and fleshy and can store _____ EWART.

4. Their _____ NSPISE keep hungry desert animals away.

5. Their bodies have a _____ XWYA covering that helps prevent water loss in the heat of the day.

6. Their _____ OROST are near the surface and spread across a large area so that they can collect water as soon as it rains.

KNOW YOUR WATER CYCLE

Evaporation, condensation and precipitation are stages of the water cycle. Can you tell which stage each of these actions falls into? Tick (✓) the correct column.

Action	Evaporation	Condensation	Precipitation
Snowfall in the mountains.			
Wet clothes drying in the sunshine.			
Droplets of water forming on the outside of a glass of iced tea.			
Rain puddles drying up in the sun.			
Clouds forming in the sky.			
A sudden shower of rain.			
Water in a saucer disappearing when left on a windowsill.			
Dew drops forming on leaves and blades of grass.			

WHAT'S THE NAME?

Human beings rear many insects, animals and plants to produce different things, and each of these means of production has a special name. Can you match the names on the left to their descriptions on the right?

pisciculture •   • the cultivation of grapes

floriculture •   • the rearing of silkworms

apiculture •   • the rearing of honeybees

sericulture •   • the rearing of earthworms

viticulture •   • the cultivation of flowers

vermiculture •   • the rearing of fish

LET'S EXPLORE

The universe is a fascinating place full of many mysteries. The more we learn about it, the more we still have left to find out! Fill in the missing letters to complete these facts and find out more about the universe we live in.

1. The planet with two moons called Phobos and Deimos is M __ __ S.

2. Earth is part of a galaxy called the M __ __ K __ W __ __.

3. The regular path that an object takes in space is an O __ __ I __.

4. The planet closest to the sun is M __ __ C __ __ Y.

5. Once a planet, P __ __ __ O is now a dwarf planet that lies in the Kuiper belt.

6. A __ __ R __ __ E D __ is the galaxy closest to Earth.

7. The small rock objects that orbit the sun between the orbits of Jupiter and Mars are called A __ __ __ R __ I __ S.

8. M E __ E O __ __ __ D S are the proper name for what we commonly call shooting stars.

ROCKS AND MINERALS

Many different types of rocks and minerals are found on and in the Earth. How well do you know them? Find these words in the grid.

lava   marble   metamorphic   granite

magma   rock   igneous   sandstone

i	m	e	t	a	m	o	r	p	h	i	c	w	v	l
j	m	n	b	d	y	y	v	q	h	q	m	y	e	p
f	z	o	n	m	q	q	w	m	g	s	b	x	e	d
j	b	t	j	m	a	g	m	a	b	b	n	l	n	m
e	h	s	w	r	i	w	a	a	u	z	b	e	e	b
m	z	a	u	w	x	g	e	s	q	k	t	t	e	g
i	c	n	z	q	b	i	n	o	n	p	l	a	v	a
f	i	d	a	p	m	r	g	e	g	m	b	j	b	c
m	o	s	p	z	b	r	z	j	o	f	q	g	d	h
a	v	t	l	y	a	o	f	r	d	u	m	v	m	y
j	h	o	v	n	m	s	p	z	c	y	s	r	a	h
w	t	n	i	g	r	a	n	i	t	e	o	l	r	s
y	y	e	n	q	i	a	n	t	n	i	d	g	b	k
j	e	s	j	c	r	q	t	p	e	y	g	b	l	m
p	n	v	z	r	o	c	k	c	r	g	o	b	e	x

Use the words you found in the grid to fill in the blanks.

1. An example of a sedimentary rock is _____.

2. A _____ is a solid made from different minerals.

3. Molten rock below the surface of the Earth is called _____.

4. _____ is an example of a metamorphic rock.

5. Molten rock that comes to the surface through a volcanic eruption is called _____.

6. Rocks formed when magma cools and solidifies are _____ rocks.

7. _____ rocks are formed because of great pressure and heat.

8. An example of an igneous rock is _____.

Darkness, the moon and a good night's sleep are some things we associate with night-time. Some birds and animals sleep during the day and are active at night. Colour the grid using the colour code to reveal a creature of the night.

Colour code:
1 – orange
2 – brown
3 – red
4 – black
5 – light blue

5	5	5	5	5	5	5	5	5	5	5	5	5	5	5	5	5	5	5	5
5	5	5	5	5	2	5	5	5	5	5	5	5	5	2	5	5	5	5	5
5	5	5	5	2	1	2	5	5	5	5	5	2	1	2	5	5	5	5	5
5	5	5	1	1	1	1	1	5	5	5	1	1	1	1	1	5	5	5	5
5	5	5	1	1	1	1	1	1	1	1	1	1	1	1	1	1	5	5	5
5	5	1	1	1				1	1	1				1	1	1	5	5	
5	1	1	1			4			1			4			1	1	1	5	
5	1	1	1		4	4		3	3	3		4	4		1	1	1	5	
5	2	1	1					3	3	3					1	1	2	5	
5	2	2	1	1				3	3	3			1	1	2	2	5		
5	2	2	2	1	1	1	1	1	3	1	1	1	1	1	2	2	2	5	
5	2	2	2	2	2	1	1	1	1	1	1	1	2	2	2	2	2	5	
5	2	2	2	2	2	1	2	1	2	1	2	1	2	2	2	2	2	5	
5	2	2	2	2	2	1	1	2	1	2	1	1	2	2	2	2	2	5	
5	5	2	2	2	1	1	1	1	2	1	1	1	1	2	2	2	5	5	
5	5	5	2	5	1	1	1	1	2	1	1	1	1	5	2	5	5	5	
5	5	5	5	5	1	1	4	1	1	1	4	1	1	5	5	5	5	5	
5	5	5	5	5	5	1	4	1	1	1	4	1	5	5	5	5	5	5	
5	5	5	5	5	5	4	4	4	5	4	4	4	5	5	5	5	5	5	
5	5	5	5	5	5	5	4	5	5	5	4	5	5	5	5	5	5	5	5
5	5	5	5	5	5	5	5	5	5	5	5	5	5	5	5	5	5	5	5

This is a/an _____. Animals that sleep during the day and are awake at night are called _____. Two other animals that do the same are _____ and _____. They are active at night to _____.

PHYSICAL OR CHEMICAL?

A pencil breaking into two pieces causes a physical change in the pencil. But when flour, eggs, butter and chocolate are mixed together and baked to form chocolate muffins, it is a chemical change. Can you tell the difference between physical changes and chemical changes? Tick (✓) the correct column for each change below.

Change	Physical	Chemical
Leaves changing their colour in autumn		
A glass breaking		
Water freezing into ice cubes		
Digesting our food		
Milk turning to curd		
Burning a candle		
A balloon bursting		
Iron nails rusting		
Baking a cake		
Melting snow		

WHO AM I?

The human body has many parts. Some of these parts, like the eyes and nose, are on the outside. Others, like the heart, are on the inside. Can you solve these riddles and identify these parts of the human body?

1 I am the longest bone in your body. Who am I?

2 I am an organ in the body with a pupil that doesn't study. Who am I?

3 I am the largest and heaviest organ in your body. Who am I?

4 The digestion of the food you eat begins here. Who am I?

5 The smallest bone in your body is located in me. Who am I?

6 I connect muscle to bone. Who am I?

7 I am the main organ of the respiratory system. Who am I?

8 I remove waste materials from the blood. Who am I?

FUEL UP!

Diesel and petrol are fossil fuels that we get from the remains of plants and animals that lived a long time ago. Plants get their energy from the sun. Draw the energy cycle below.

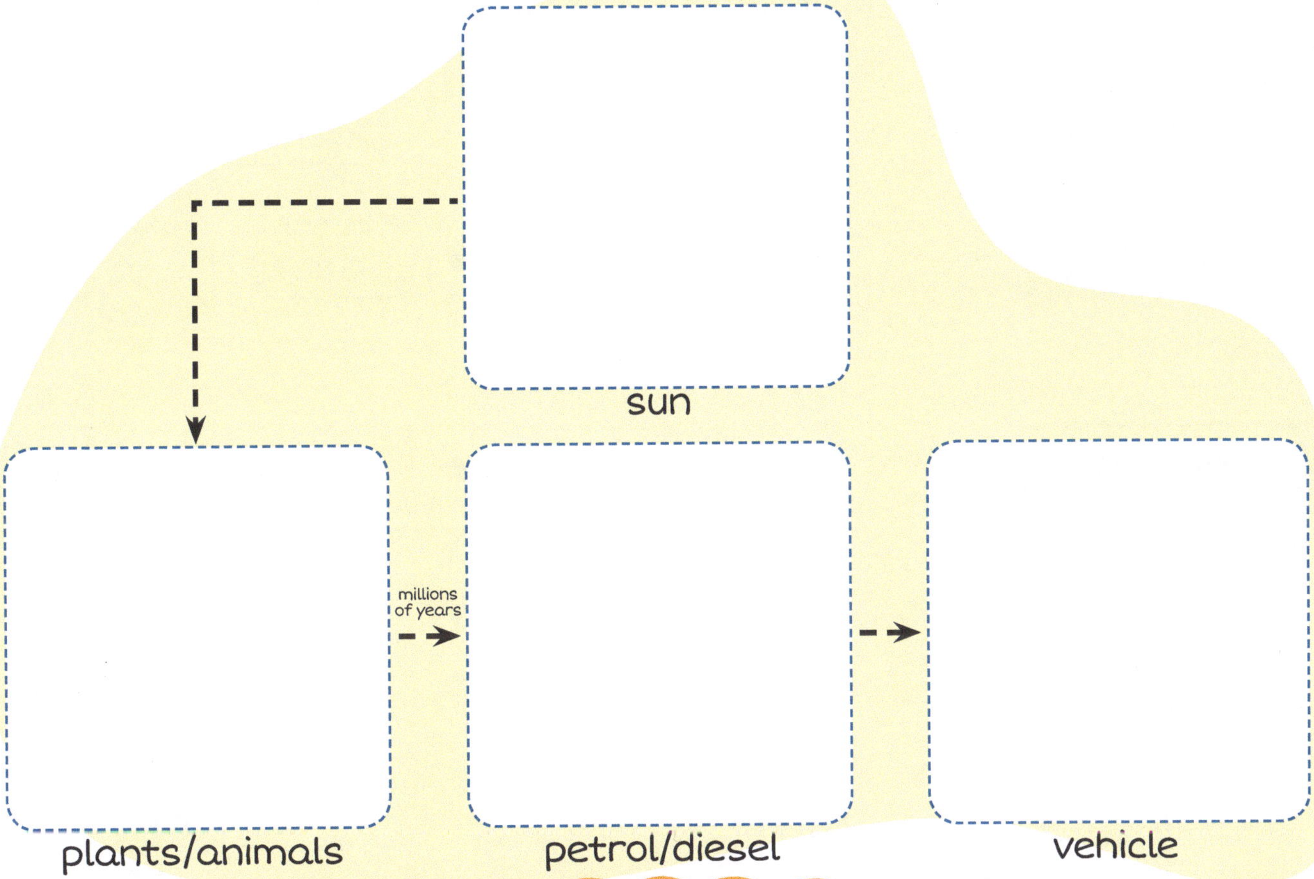

sun

plants/animals

millions of years

petrol/diesel

vehicle

_____ is another fossil fuel. We use it for

_____.

SEED TRAVELS

If seeds fell under the parent plant they would have to compete with each other for water and nutrients. This is why seeds are sent far away through a process called dispersal. There are many modes of dispersal. Match each seed below to the mode of dispersal it relies on.

Type of seed

Agent of dispersal

coconut

air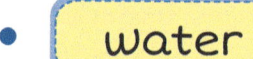

guava

water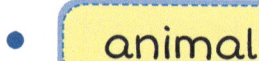

dandelion

animal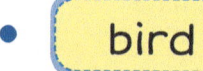

pea

bird

sand burr

explosion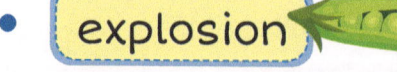

If you were a plant, what mode of dispersal would you want to rely on? Design a seed and explain how it is dispersed.

Draw here.

_____

_____

_____

LET IT SNOW

Snow, like rain, is a form of precipitation. Each snowflake has a unique shape. Can you match each snowflake to its identical twin?

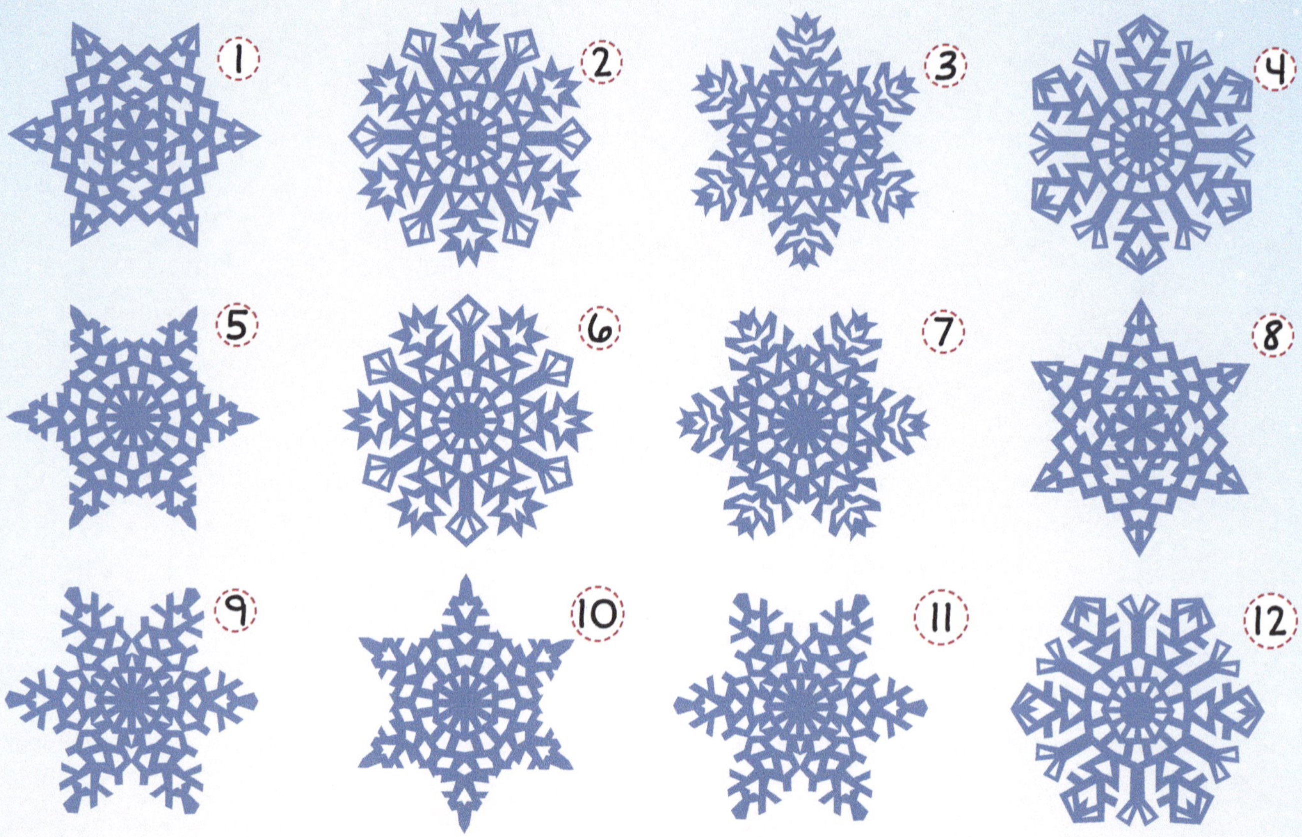

① ② ③ ④

⑤ ⑥ ⑦ ⑧

⑨ ⑩ ⑪ ⑫

Snowflakes are formed at freezing temperatures when water vapour condenses on tiny bits of _____ to form ice _____. These stick together to form snowflakes.

WE CARE

Planet Earth is our home. We need to protect it for ourselves and for future generations as well. Write or draw different ways in which we can show that we care for the environment.

At home

At school

At a picnic

In our neighbourhood

WHERE'S YOUR BACKBONE?

What's one difference between you and a jellyfish? You have a backbone, a jellyfish doesn't. Write down each animal name in the box in the correct column.

squid   scorpion   barnacle   iguana   flamingo
tarantula   salamander   meerkat   slug   macaw

Vertebrate (has a backbone)	Invertebrate (has no backbone)

PARTICLE MATTERS

Solid, liquid and gaseous are different states of matter. All matter is made up of tiny particles. Identify which state of matter the following items are in by colouring them according to the code below.

Solid – ⬤ Liquid – ⬤ Gas – ⬤

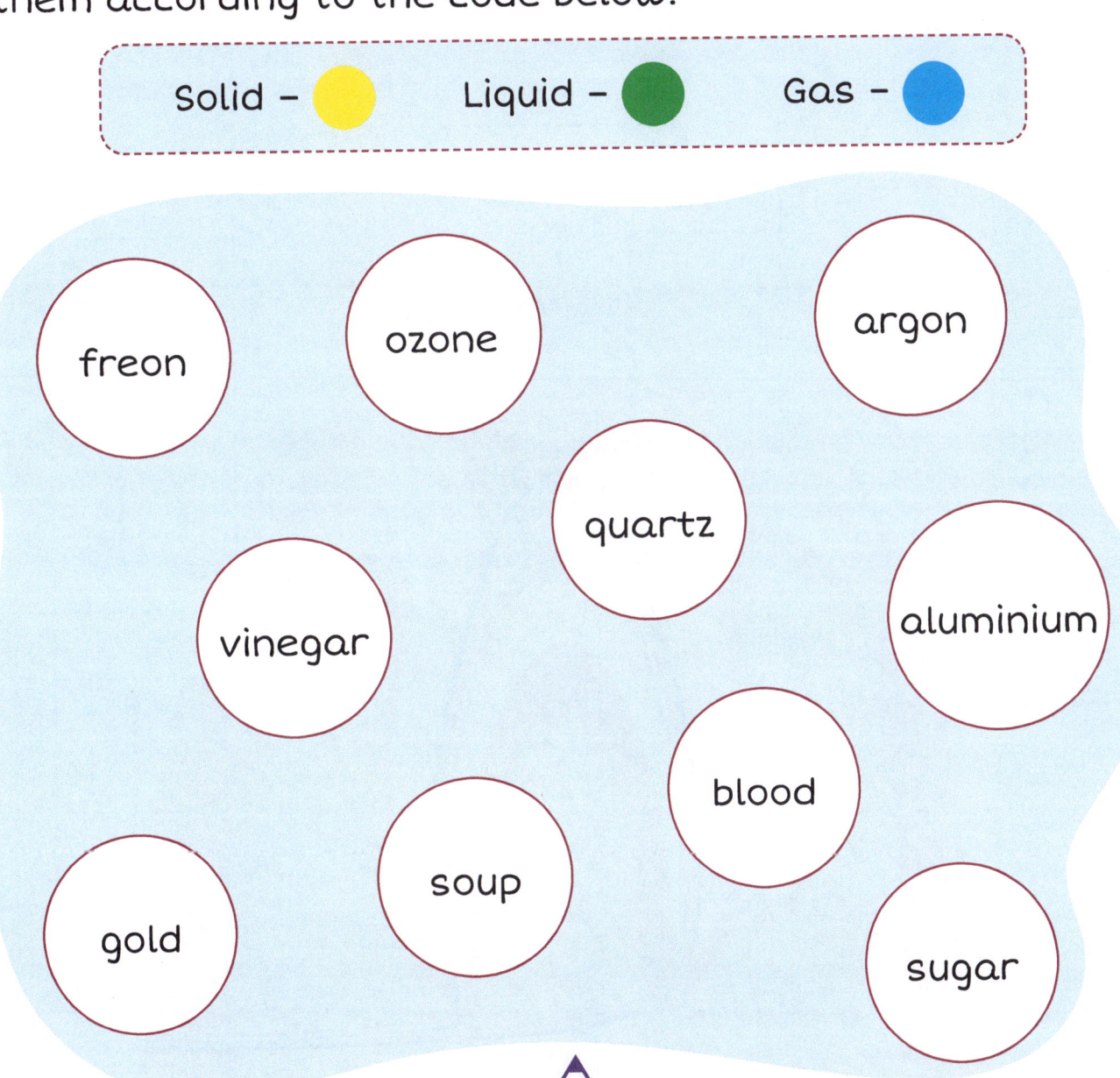

freon

ozone

argon

quartz

vinegar

aluminium

blood

soup

gold

sugar

TOOTH TRUTHS

How well do you know your teeth? Label the diagram below with words from the box.

gums   crown   root   enamel   pulp   dentine

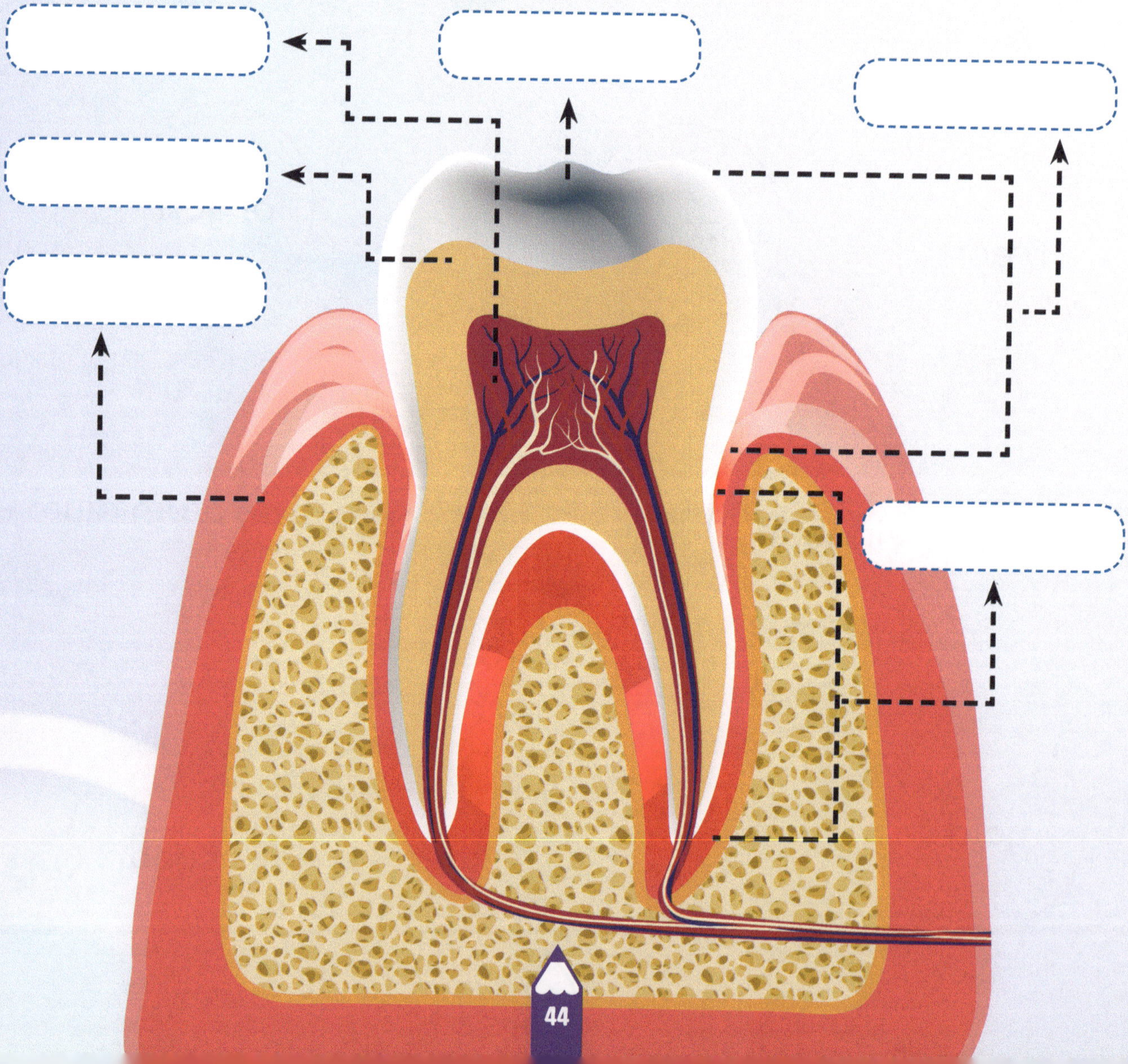

Fill in the blanks with words from the box.

1. I am the part of your tooth above the gum. Who am I?

2. I am soft and have blood vessels and nerves running through me. Who am I?

3. I am the hardest substance in the body. Who am I?

4. I am the bit embedded into the jawbone. Who am I?

5. I am harder than bone and form the bulk of your tooth. Who am I?

6. Your teeth start growing through me when you are a tiny baby. Who am I?

BE NATURAL

The first step to recycling is separating biodegradable waste from non-biodegradable waste. Can you tell the difference between them? Tick (✓) the correct column for each waste item.

Waste	Biodegradable (waste from plants and animals that can be decomposed)	Non-biodegradable (cannot be broken down or decomposed)
tin can		
old newspaper		
tea leaves		
plastic container		
feathers		
eggshells		
batteries		
food waste		
cotton rags		
broken glass		

HEALTHY METHODS

Cooking is fun but we can sometimes reduce the amount of nutrients in our food because we use the wrong cooking methods. Identify the rights and wrongs of cooking methods by putting a tick (✔) in the correct column.

	🙂	☹️
Washing vegetables before cutting them.		
Cooking rice in more water than needed.		
Adding a lot of salt to food.		
Washing of food grains like rice too many times before cooking.		
Using a moderate amount of oil while cooking.		
Overcooking vegetables and meats.		
Preserving cooked food in the refrigerator.		
Eating a whole fruit instead of making it into fruit juice or milkshakes.		

BREATHE IN

We all need oxygen to survive. Filtering oxygen from the air we breathe in is the job of our respiratory system. How well do you know your respiratory system? Fill in the missing letters to find out.

1. The __ __ __ G __ are the pair of organs in which the exchange of gases takes place.

2. The T __ A __ __ E __ is a part of the body that is also called the windpipe.

3. The sheet of muscle below your lungs is the D __ __ P __ R __ G __.

4. The clusters of tiny balloon-like sacs at the end of the bronchioles are the A __ V __ __ L __.

5. The L __ __ Y __ X is also known as the voice box.

6. The branches of the trachea that enter the lungs are the __ R __ N __ H __.

GASES GALORE

Gases are everywhere, yet we don't even know they are there. All living things on the planet depend on these gases to do different things. Match the gas to its description.

neon   •

oxygen   •

helium   •

nitrogen   •

carbon dioxide   •

ozone   •

nitrous oxide   •

• Plants use it to make their food.

• This is also known as laughing gas.

• The most abundant gas in the atmosphere.

• A gas used to illuminate billboards.

• This protects Earth from the sun's harmful UV rays.

• It is used to fill up balloons.

• Living organisms need it to survive.

ENERGY FORMS

Heat, sound and light are different forms of energy. Some objects produce only heat, light or sound, some produce two of these, while some produce all three! Tick (✓) the correct column or columns depending on the type of energy produced by these objects.

Object		Heat	Sound	Light
doorbell				
mobile				
toaster				
television				
wood fire				
crackers				
electric guitar				
candle				

50

A frying pan is usually made of a combination of different materials. The pan may be made of metal while the handle may be made of a material that is heat resistant. Choose two objects that you see around you. Fill in the table below with information about them and draw them in the spaces below.

Name	Use	Material/s made from	Why the material was used

BRILLIANT BUGS

Beetles and bugs form one of the largest groups of insects in the world. Many are a source of food for other creatures like frogs and lizards. Spot ten differences between these two images.

Cochineal is a _____ coloured food dye extracted from the _____.

52

NOT SO SIMPLE

Simple machines are tools that we use to work more easily and efficiently. We use them all the time: a pair of scissors, a can opener, etc. We even have simple machines like see-saws on our playgrounds! Draw a simple machine that you use at home, at school and on the playground in the spaces below.

Home

School

Playground

CREATING CONSTELLATIONS

Constellations are groups of stars that appear to form patterns in the sky. All through history, people have looked at these patterns and named them after people, animals or mythological figures. Can you match the constellations below to their names?

Constellation

Common name

Aries

The Harp

Cancer

The Ram

Pegasus

The Crab

Lyra

The Winged Horse

Constellations look like giant join-the-dots puzzles in the night sky. Look up at the sky at night. Create your own constellation in the space below.

Draw here.

The name of my constellation is _____.

It looks like a _____.

ATTRACTION EXPLAINED

When two magnets are brought near each other they either stick to each other like glue or push away from each other. How much do you know about magnets? Let's find out. Label the poles of these magnets.

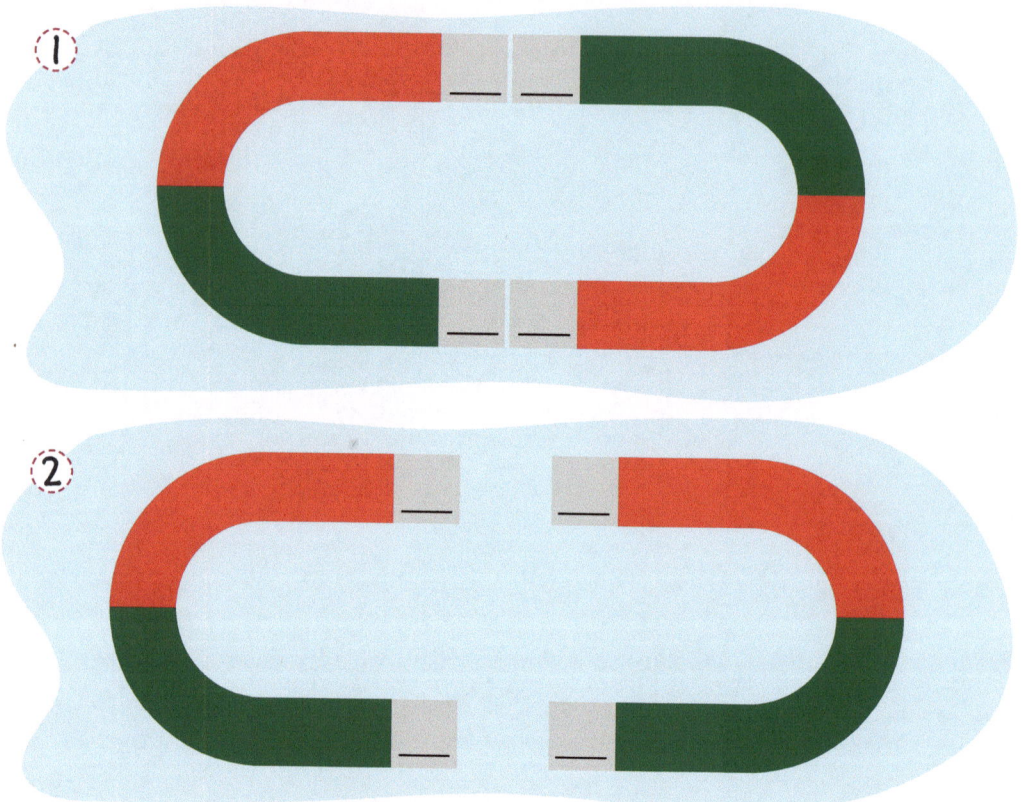

All magnets have two poles: a _____ pole and a _____ pole. Like poles _____ each other. Unlike poles _____ each other.

POWER SOURCE

Most of the gadgets that we use in our homes require electricity to work, but there are some that don't! Can you identify the source of power needed to run these gadgets? Tick (✓) the correct column.

Gadget	Electricity	Battery	No power needed
washing machine			
torch			
cycle			
wristwatch			
mixer			
toaster			
hammer			
calculator			
scissors			

WATER HOMES

A habitat is a place where a plant or an animal lives. Habitats can be terrestrial (on land) or aquatic (in the water). Draw lines to connect all the plants that live in an aquatic habitat to the central circle.

water lily

orchid

sunflower

duckweed

oak

Aquatic habitat

algae

water hyacinth

lotus

sea weed

Draw a plant that lives in an aquatic habitat.

Draw here.

Name the plant: _____. How is this plant

adapted to live in water?_____

_____.

ANSWERS

page 4 WHAT'S EDIBLE?
potato; beet; cauliflower; pear; pineapple; turnip

page 5 MATCH ME!
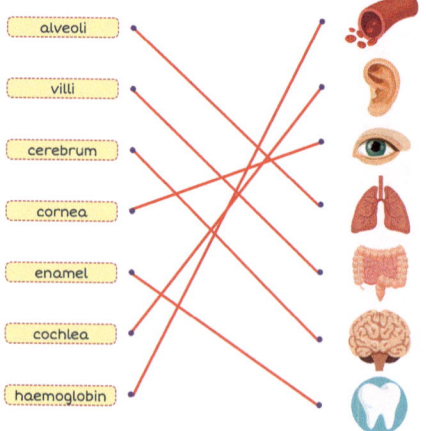

alveoli
villi
cerebrum
cornea
enamel
cochlea
haemoglobin

page 6 SENSATIONAL SENSES
Sight: colour, beauty; Hearing: music, whisper, thunder; Taste: salty, bitter; Touch: smooth, rough; Smell: odour

page 7 RAINBOW FOODS
Answers may vary.

Look this up: Answers will be based on the child's research.

page 8–9 WATCH THEM GROW!
Look this up: Answers will be based on the child's research.

Answers may vary.

page 10 INSECT WATCH
Answers may vary.

page 11 SAFETY FIRST

Situation	Description	Why is it dangerous?
	A child playing with a matchbox and fire	We could burn ourselves.
	A child accepting a sweet from a stranger	Strangers and unknown persons can kidnap us and take us away from our family.
CAUTION WET FLOOR	Playing/running on a wet floor	We could slip, fall and hurt ourselves.
	Children putting their hands out of a moving vehicle	We could injure ourselves.

Descriptions may vary, but answers should be acceptable if similar.

page 12 DIFFERENT COVERS

	Fur	Feathers	Scales	Shell	Spines
emu		✓			
tortoise				✓	
tiger	✓				
flamingo		✓			
hedgehog					✓
fish			✓		
snail				✓	
cobra			✓		
polar bear	✓				
porcupine					✓

page 13 MATERIAL MAGIC
1. hardest; 2. tough; 3. soft; 4. brittle; 5. flexible, stiff; 6. absorbs; 7. waterproof

page 14 TASTING TIME
Look this up: Answers will be based on the child's research.

page 15 FRICTION!

Surface	More/Less Friction
smooth floor	less
lawn	more
pavement	more
carpet	more
glass table top	less

Answers may vary in the observation chart. 1. less; 2. more

page 16 WHAT YOU EAT
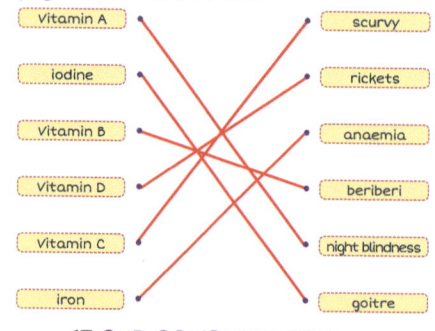

Vitamin A
iodine
Vitamin B
Vitamin D
Vitamin C
iron

scurvy
rickets
anaemia
beriberi
night blindness
goitre

page 17 OUR COMPLEX BODY
2. liver; 3. heart; 4. wrist; 5. kidney; 6. liver; 7. knee

page 18 KNOW YOUR PLANTS
ACROSS: 4. FRUIT; 5. CHLOROPHYLL; 6. LEAVES

DOWN: 1. ROOTS; 2. STOMATA; 3. POLLEN; 4. FLOWER

page 19 AM I EATING HEALTHY?
Answers may vary.

Look this up: Answers will be based on the child's research.

page 20 HOUSE BUILDERS

c	a	q	i	m	b	r	i	c	k	s	w	o	o	d
h	i	c	c	t	j	g	k	y	k	i	x	r	v	x
s	o	q	h	k	o	g	p	u	g	p	i	c	m	p
z	i	v	y	u	f	p	g	l	a	s	s	h	z	l
w	p	p	x	r	a	m	n	f	l	l	q	b	n	a
m	f	i	w	l	b	j	a	r	j	x	o	o	h	s
a	x	k	o	p	r	g	z	m	p	k	n	r	a	t
r	a	n	j	m	i	b	h	l	c	c	p	w	l	i
b	s	c	o	n	c	r	e	t	e	r	l	n	u	c
l	e	h	x	m	w	o	d	t	s	n	j	m	o	o
e	f	y	x	i	p	v	g	t	t	s	n	i	m	x
t	r	u	y	q	j	h	y	u	m	h	u	n	u	d
o	e	z	p	q	d	u	h	t	y	m	y	i	d	d
o	s	t	e	e	l	w	f	q	x	u	s	h	u	x
i	c	e	k	l	q	u	n	q	z	r	p	m	d	d

page 21 HOUSE BUILDERS
wood: doors, windows, furniture; concrete: walls, flooring; steel: walls, furniture; aluminium: window frames; bricks: walls; plastic: chairs; fabric: curtains, furnishings; marble: flooring, kitchen counters; glass: windows

page 22 POSTER TIME
Answers may vary.

page 23 NOT QUITE ALIVE

	Non-living characteristics	Conditions required for transformation	Living characteristics after the change
Egg	Cannot move, feed, excrete or react to the changes in its environment	Warmth of the mother's feathers (temperature)	A baby bird can now move, feed, excrete or react to the changes in its environment.
Seed	Cannot move, make its own food or react to the changes in its environment	Air, water, sunlight (temperature), soil	A tiny plant can move, make its own food or react to the changes in its environment.

page 24–25 CANDLELIGHT

	Observation	Inference (Why did the candle continue to burn/not burn?)
Candle 1	Continues to burn	It continued to burn because of the presence of oxygen in the air.
Candle 2	Goes off after sometime	It went off after a while because the oxygen in the air in the bell jar was depleted.

page 26 ARE WE ALIKE?
Answers may vary.

page 27 COLOURFUL CORAL

Underwater organisms in the picture: fish, sea turtle, crab, starfish sea horse, coral

Great Barrier Reef, Australia

page 28 CLEVER CACTUS
1. LEAVES; 2. PHOTOSYNTHESIS;
3. WATER; 4. SPINES; 5. WAXY;
6. ROOTS

page 29 KNOW YOUR WATER CYCLE

Scenario	Evaporation	Condensation	Precipitation
Snowfall in the mountains.			✓
Wet clothes drying in the sunshine.	✓		
Droplets of water forming on the outside of a glass of iced tea.		✓	
Rain puddles drying up in the sun.	✓		
Clouds forming in the sky.		✓	
A sudden shower of rain.			✓
Water in a saucer disappearing when left on a windowsill.	✓		
Dew drops forming on leaves and blades of grass.		✓	

page 30 WHAT'S THE NAME?

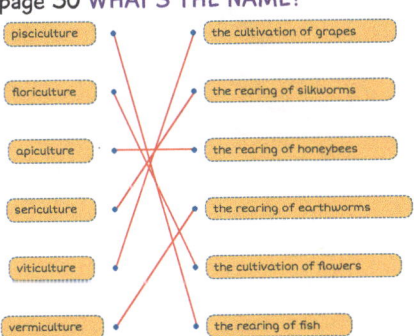

pisciculture — the cultivation of grapes
floriculture — the rearing of silkworms
apiculture — the rearing of honeybees
sericulture — the rearing of earthworms
viticulture — the cultivation of flowers
vermiculture — the rearing of fish

page 31 LET'S EXPLORE
1. MARS; 2. MILKY WAY; 3. ORBIT;
4. MERCURY; 5. PLUTO;
6. ANDROMEDA; 7. ASTEROIDS;
8. METEOROIDS

page 32 ROCKS AND MINERALS

page 33 ROCKS AND MINERALS
1. sandstone; 2. rock; 3. magma;
4. marble; 5. lava; 6. igneous;
7. metamorphic; 8. granite

page 34 NIGHT WATCHMAN

owl; nocturnal; bat, fox, raccoon, wolf (some nocturnal animals); hunt, feed escape from the heat, escape from predators

page 35 PHYSICAL OR CHEMICAL?

Changes	Physical	Chemical
Leaves changing their colour in autumn		✓
A glass breaking	✓	
Water freezing into ice cubes	✓	
Digesting our food		✓
Milk turning to curd		✓
Burning a candle		✓
A balloon bursting	✓	
Iron nails rusting		✓
Baking a cake		✓
Melting snow	✓	

page 36 WHO AM I?
1. femur; 2. eye; 3. skin; 4. mouth; 5. ear;
6. tendon; 7. lungs; 8. kidney

page 37 FUEL UP!
Coal is another fossil fuel. We use it for cooking, heating, making electricity, etc

page 38–39 SEED TRAVELS

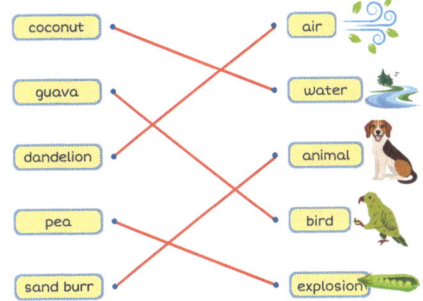

coconut — water
guava — animal
dandelion — air
pea — explosion
sand burr — bird

Answers may vary for the second part.

page 40 LET IT SNOW
1–8, 2–6, 3–7, 4–12, 5–10, 9–11

dust or dirt or chemicals; crystals

page 41 WE CARE
Answers may vary.

page 42 WHERE'S YOUR BACKBONE?
Vertebrate: iguana, flamingo, salamander, meerkat, macaw

Invertebrate: squid, scorpion, barnacle, tarantula, slug

page 43 PARTICLE MATTERS

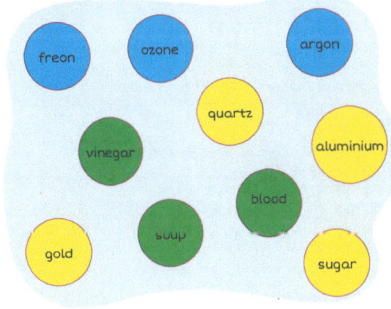

page 44 TOOTH TRUTHS

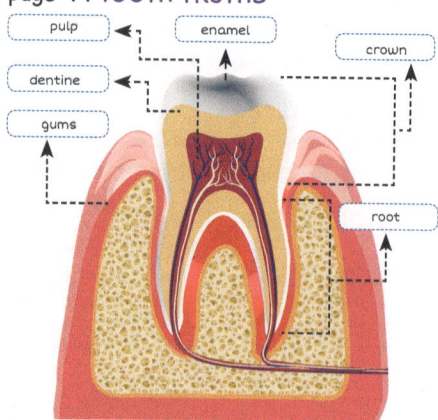

pulp, enamel, crown, dentine, gums, root

page 45 TOOTH TRUTHS
1. crown; 2. pulp; 3. enamel; 4. root;
5. dentine; 6. gums

page 46 BE NATURAL

Waste	Biodegradable (waste from plants and animals that can be decomposed)	Non-biodegradable (cannot be broken down or decomposed)
tin can		✓
old newspaper	✓	
tea leaves	✓	
plastic container		✓
feathers	✓	
eggshells	✓	
batteries		✓
food waste	✓	
cotton rags	✓	
broken glass		✓

page 47 HEALTHY METHODS

	☺	☹
Washing vegetables before cutting them.	✓	
Cooking rice in more water than needed.		✓
Adding a lot of salt to food.		✓
Washing of food grains like rice too many times before cooking.		✓
Using a moderate amount of oil while cooking.	✓	
Overcooking vegetables and meats.		✓
Preserving cooked food in the refrigerator.	✓	
Eating a whole fruit instead of making it into fruit juice or milkshakes.	✓	

page 48 BREATHE IN
1. LUNGS; 2. TRACHEA;
3. DIAPHRAGM; 4. ALVEOLI;
5. LARYNX; 6. BRONCHI

page 49 GASES GALORE
neon—A gas used to illuminate
billboards; oxygen—Living organisms
need it to survive; helium—It is used to fill
up balloons; nitrogen—The most abundant
gas in the atmosphere; carbon dioxide—
Plants use it to make their food; ozone—
This protects Earth from the sun's harmful
UV rays; nitrous oxide—This is also known
as laughing gas.

page 50 ENERGY FORMS

Object		Heat	Sound	Light
doorbell			✓	
mobile			✓	✓
toaster		✓		
television				✓
wood fire		✓		✓
crackers		✓	✓	✓
electric guitar			✓	
candle		✓		✓

page 51 MATERIAL CHECK
Answers may vary.

page 52 BRILLIANT BUGS

red, insects

page 53 NOT SO SIMPLE
Answers may vary.

page 54 CREATING CONSTELLATIONS

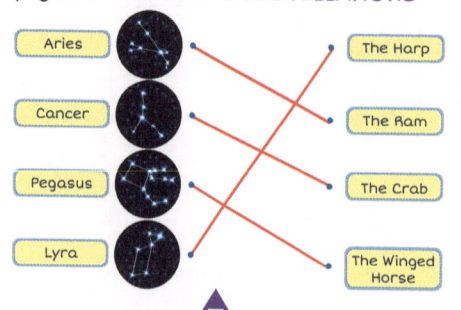

Aries — The Ram
Cancer — The Crab
Pegasus — The Winged Horse
Lyra — The Harp

page 55 CREATING CONSTELLATIONS
Answers may vary.

page 56 ATRRACTION EXPLAINED

① N S / S N

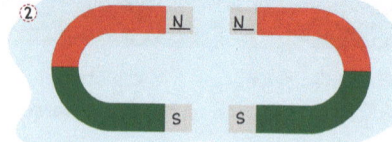

② N N / S S

north, south, repel, attract

page 57 POWER SOURCE

Gadget	Electricity	Battery	No power needed
washing machine	✓		
torch		✓	
cycle			✓
wristwatch		✓	
mixer	✓		
toaster	✓		
hammer			✓
calculator		✓	
scissors			✓

page 58 WATER HOMES

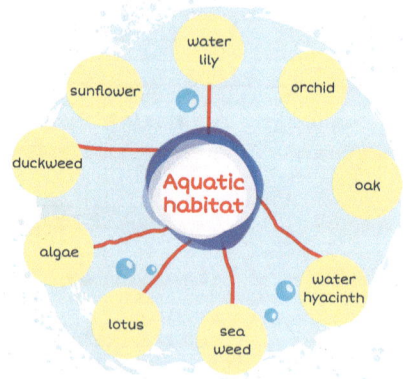

Aquatic habitat: water lily, orchid, oak, water hyacinth, sea weed, lotus, algae, duckweed, sunflower

page 59 WATER HOMES
Answers may vary.